Second Simple Recipes for Little Kids and Adults

By Sarah Mason

Copyright ©2020 by Sarah Mason

All rights reserved. Printed in the United States of America. No part of this book may be used or reproduced in any manner whatsoever without written permission except in the case of brief quotations embodied in critical articles and reviews.

For more information please contact at simplerecipecookbooks@gmail.com.

ISBN: 978-0-578-75406-2

Contents

Introduction	7
Starters	9
Mains	15
Sides	21
Desserts	24

Introduction

Healthy eating is important at all ages. Moderation and portions are important. From my experiences, asking what my child should eat never came back with a good answer. What we feed children uses portions smaller than for an adult according to professional guidance. Over time, I have found recipes that are fulfilling small eaters and big eater.

This book is the second book of the series and has no meat recipes. No meat recipes, or poultry are included. This book is an easy way to make a meal with dairy that includes starter, main, sides, and desserts that everyone will enjoy.

Starters

Greens Salad with Oil dressing

Ingredients
Raw Romaine Lettuce
Raw butter lettuce
Raw green pepper
¼ c light olive oil
1 tbs white vinegar
¼ tsp granulated sugar
Pinch salt
Pinch black pepper

Directions
Salad
Wash and pat the greens dry with a paper towel
Tear the lettuces into small pieces by hand
Cut the pepper by removing top and seeds, slicing the vegetable into strips
Combine vegetables
Dressing
Mix oil, vinegar, granulated sugar, salt, and pepper
Drizzle on salad

Purple Plated Salad

Ingredients
8.25oz can sliced beets
8oz bag shredded purple cabbage
Light Olive Oil
Pinch salt
Pinch Black Pepper

Directions
Salad
Pour out half bag of purple cabbage onto plate
Empty can of beets and rinse and slice
into strips, place on top of cabbage on plate
Dressing
Mix oil with the pepper and salt
Pour dressing on plated salad

Onion Soup

Ingredients

4 medium sweet onions
4 tbs butter
¼ c red cooking wine
½ tbs salt
¼ tsp pepper
4 c water

Directions

Prepare onions by removing skin, halving, and slicing into rounds
Heat butter in bottom of a pot using medium heat on stove
Put salt and pepper in butter mix
Add onions, sauté until onions are soft
Add water and red wine
Cook covered on stove for 45 minutes

Tomato Soup

Ingredients

28oz can petite diced tomato
1c water
1 tsp Salt
¼ tsp Pepper
¼ c Vinegar
½ tsp Oregano
¼ tsp Basil

Directions

Combine all ingredients in large pot
Bring to a simmer
Cook covered for 20 minutes
Remove soup in batches and puree with a hand blender
Return soup to pot
When at desired thickness, stop batches

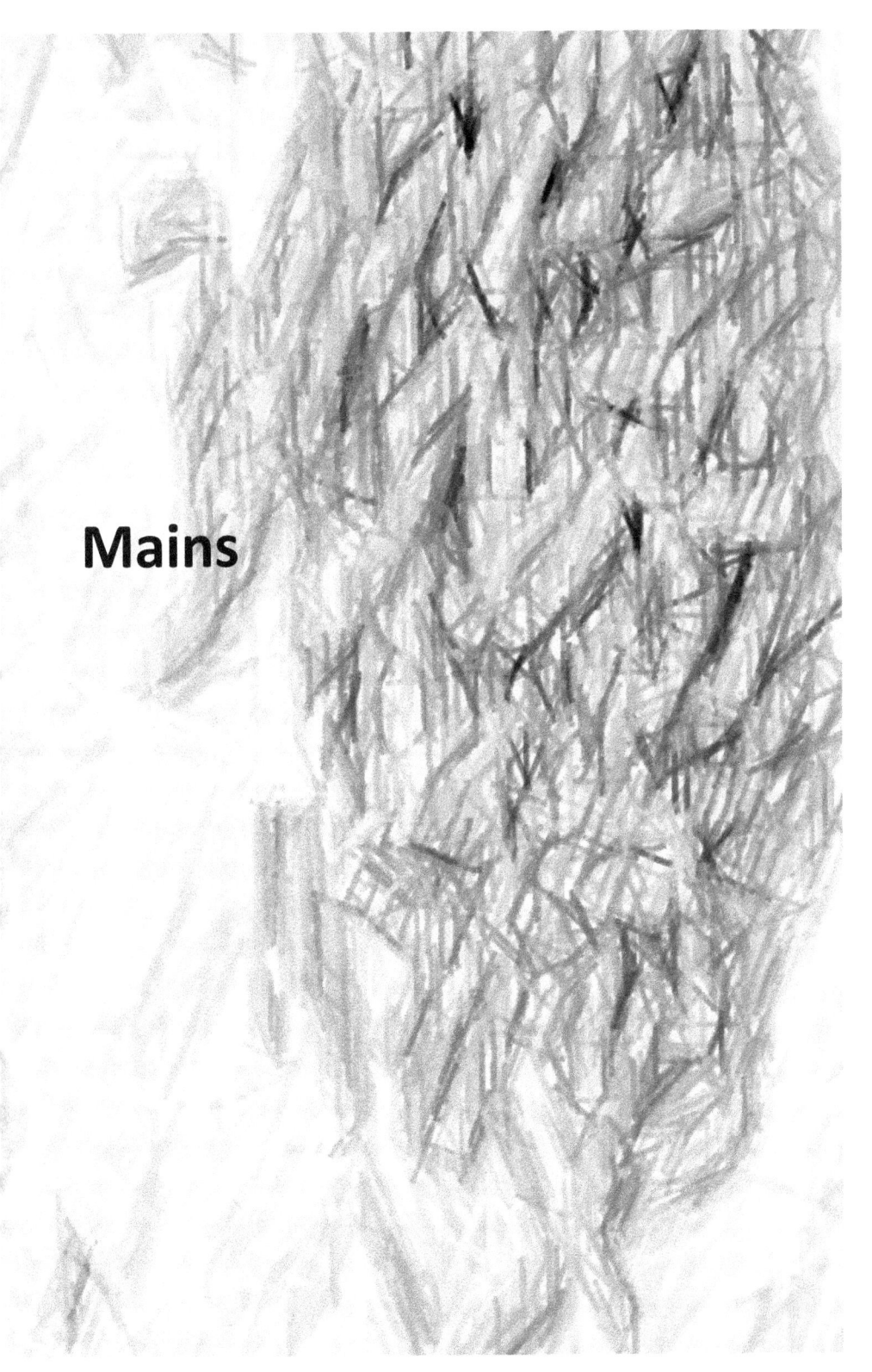

Mains

Dairy Taco

Ingredients
4 soft corn tortillas
1c vegan meat crumbles
1 packet taco seasoning
Diced tomatoes (Optional)
Shredded lettuce (Optional)
Shredded cheese (Optional)
Sour cream (Optional)

Directions
Warm corn tortillas in 350 oven for 7 minutes
Warm meat crumbles in skillet with water
Add taco seasoning, stir
After water is thickened, remove from stove
Take one tortilla, one scoop of "meat"
and tomato, lettuce, cheese, and sour cream
on one half of tortilla
Fold over tortilla

Baked Pasta

Ingredients
1 box regular or gluten-free penne pasta
8oz ricotta
1 ½ c shredded mozzarella
1 jar marinara

Directions
Cook pasta according to directions
Drain, place in large bowl
In bowl, add ricotta, mozzarella, and jar of
marinara
Pour mixture into a pan
Place mozzarella onto pasta in pan
Bake at 350 for 25 minutes

Pasta with Green Vegetables
Ingredients
1 box rotini
½ c frozen peas
½ c frozen spinach
1 c ricotta
Salt
Pepper

Directions
Cook box of rotini according to directions with peas in pot
Drain
Add frozen spinach and stir for 2-3 minutes
Add ricotta, salt, and pepper to tase and stir for 3 minutes

Fried Fish

Ingredients
4 medium tilapia fillets
2 eggs, beaten
1c Cornflake crumbs
1c Pancake mix
Oil

Directions
Place eggs in a wide shallow bowl
Place cornflake crumbs and Pancake mix on a large plate combine with hands
Take a tilapia fillet and break into four pieces
Each piece is dredged in egg, then dry mixture
4 pieces of tilapia at a time are fried in hot oil in a pan on stove
Remove from oil when browned and firm
Place on a paper towel lined plate to drain extra oil from fish

Sides

Fast Cole Slaw
Ingredients: 2c shredded cabbage, ½ c mayonnaise, 1 tbs lemon juice, salt, and pepper
Directions: Mix cabbage, mayonnaise, lemon juice, salt, and pepper in a bowl. Add 1 tsp sugar into bowl. Let rest in refrigerator 1 hour before serving

Sweet Carrots
Ingredients: 1lb carrots, ¼ c honey, ¼ tsp salt, ¼ tsp cinnamon, and oil
Directions: Peel and cut carrots into wheels. Place carrots and oil in pan, sauté over medium heat until soft. Turn off heat. In warm pan, add honey, cinnamon, and salt. Stir.

Roasted Squash
Ingredients: 1 medium butternut squash, salt, pepper, and oil
Directions: Peel and cut squash into pieces. Place squash in a 9x12 pan. Drizzle with oil and add salt and pepper to taste. Place in oven 55 minutes at 400

Potato Wedges

Ingredients: 4 large russet potatoes, oil, salt, and pepper

Directions: Peel and cut potatoes into wedges. Place potatoes in a 9x12 pan. Drizzle with oil. Add salt and pepper to taste. Place in oven 55 minutes at 400

Quick Breadstix

Ingredients: Prepackaged pizza dough, 2 tsp garlic powder, 2 tsp salt

Directions: Cut thawed prepackaged pizza dough into 12 pieces. Take each piece and form into a piece of rope. Place each rope on a cookie sheet. Sprinkle with mix of salt and garlic powder. Place in oven according to directions for pizza dough

Desserts

Mini Fruit Kabob

Ingredients
1 large banana
1 c blueberries
2 c cubed watermelon
toothpicks

Directions
Peel and cut banana into thick wheels
Wash and dry blueberries
Take one toothpick and put one banana wheel, one blueberry, and one piece of watermelon. Repeat until ingredients are done

Chocolate Chip Cookies

Ingredients
¾ c granulated sugar
1c brown sugar, packed
¾ c oil
2 eggs
2 tsp vanilla
2 ½ c all-purpose flour or gluten free blend
¾ tsp baking soda
6 oz chocolate chips
½ c chopped pecans (Optional)

Directions
Mix oil, eggs, and vanilla in a large bowl
Add granulated and brown sugar to bowl
and stir until smooth
Add flour and baking soda to bowl.
Stir to combine
Add chocolate chips and pecans and mix
Take dough and form small balls about an inch diameter
Place balls on cookie sheet with 2in between and flattening slightly
Place sheets in oven at 350 for 8 minutes and leave on sheet for 10 minutes to cool before removing

Brownie with Cookies

Ingredients

1 ½ c all-purpose flour or gluten free blend
1c white sugar
1 egg
¾ c oil
½ tsp vanilla extract
½ c cocoa powder
¾ tsp baking powder
¼ c water
½ c crushed cookies, chocolate chip or sandwich

Directions

In a large bowl, mix all wet ingredients
Add sugar to wet ingredients and stir to combine
Add flour, cocoa, and baking powder. Stir until smooth
Add cookie crumbles mix well
Pour into an 8x8 pan and bake 50 min at 350

Chocolate Cupcakes

Ingredients

1 ¾ c all-purpose flour or gluten free blend
1c white sugar
3 egg
¼ c oil
¾ c rice or soy milk
½ tsp vanilla extract
½ c cocoa powder
¾ tsp baking powder
½ tsp baking soda
1 can vanilla frosting

Directions

In a large bowl, mix all wet ingredients
Add sugar to wet ingredients and stir to combine
Add flour, cocoa, baking powder, and baking soda. Stir until smooth
Pour into a muffin pan and bake 40 min at 350
Let cool for 2-3 hours. Ice with vanilla frosting

www.ingramcontent.com/pod-product-compliance
Lightning Source LLC
Chambersburg PA
CBHW031440040426
42444CB00006B/905